Forgiveness is Not an Option
The Dawn of a New Day

By Helga A. Clarke

Heart Thoughts Publishing
Floyds Knobs, IN

Printed in the United States of America

First Printing, 2014

ISBN-13: 978-1500360641
ISBN-10: 1500360643

Contact: Pastor Helga Clarke
PastorHelga@hfimt.org
(305) 620-2986

Heart Thoughts Publishing
P.O. Box 536
Floyds Knobs, IN 47119

Dedication

I dedicate this book to the masses that are struggling with unforgiveness. May you understand the power that lies within you to make changes in your life that will positively affect your destiny.

Endorsements

"Wow! This book is medicine for the broken heart. It's for anyone who has been hurt or betrayed by another and is seeking therapy and recovery back to joyful living."

Bishop Donald F. Clarke, Senior Pastor,
Harvest Fire Worship Center, Miami, FL
CEO of Asset Based Lending Consultants and Don Clarke Enterprises, Hollywood, FL

"If you are truly ready to be free from the bondage of unforgiveness, allow Pastor Clarkes' words to minister to your soul. Your freedom awaits."

Rev. Vanessa Collins
Intensive Faith Ministries International
Vanessa Collins LLC

Acknowledgements

I am truly grateful to My Lord and Savior, Jesus Christ, for the opportunity granted me, to write what He has walked me through. I give Him all the praise and the glory for not withholding from me what I needed to succeed and to live an overcoming life.

To my husband, by friend, by darling, the love of my life, Bishop Donald Clarke, I thank you so much for the gentle nudge when I got too busy to concentrate on writing. I love you so much for your love, your patience, and your encouragements. You are the best.

My four wonderful children, Keturah, Donald Jr., Simone, Dwight; my beautiful Daughters in Love; Tanieka and Melissa; my great Son in Love, Daniel Roman and all my grandchildren. I love you all with all my heart. You have taught me what true forgiveness looks like.

To those who have encouraged me, believed in me and motivated me to keep writing, you know who you are; I thank you! You have helped to make this possible. May you all be eternally blessed.

And last, but not least, to my book coach, mentor, motivator, Vanessa Collins, who entered my life when I almost gave up, your calls, your texts, emails and gentle persuasions made this possible to be in print. Thank you!

Table of Contents

Introduction

Several years ago I encountered a situation in my life, brought on by someone in whom I trusted which caused me much pain. I remember the hurt of betrayal and wrongful accusation. I could not imagine anyone being so ferocious; especially one I have had a close working relationship with and shared Christian fellowship together. I could not understand the onslaught. So deep was the pain that praying seemed impossible. I literally knelt by my bed groaning and crying buckets of tears. I wanted to know what I had done, for this to happen. I knelt there for what seemed like hours.

I thought of my accuser and wondered how could she? Everything in me wanted to lash out against her. So much emotion was taking place on the inside. I wanted to face my accuser. I was angry and upset. I kept mumbling, "I must forgive," but I did not feel like it. Not understanding then that forgiveness has nothing to do with feeling. I kept this hurt to myself. I chose not to divulge to any other person what I was going through. I did not, at that time want to hear any other voice. Later, I was glad I did not hear other voices, I believe it might have dwarfed what God wanted to accomplish in me.

There are times, when silence is golden. Had I gotten another person involved, in the embryonic stage of the challenges I was going through, it might have damaged or aborted the plan that God had for me, even in this worst-case scenario. For that I am grateful. It is noteworthy to say, that even in the darkest moments of your life, God has a plan. Nothing is wasted, no matter how bad the situation; God will turn what seemed so dismal into something praise-worthy for His glory. I was thankful too that I did not have to deal with the voice of well-meaning others, who might have had good intentions to console me, but rather might have led me down the wrong path with wrong advice.

Still kneeing there by my bedside, I opened my Bible randomly, I just needed something for my hurting soul. The first Scripture I remember was Isaiah chapter 54. I remember reading the first verse with a question mark in my mind, but I kept reading and "Walla!" verse 17. "No weapon formed against thee shall prosper." I continued reading on through several chapters. There were such precious promises for me to cling. "When you passed through the waters, I will be with you;" I was reminded that I "should not fear," for He is upholding me with His righteous right hand. There were so many beautiful scriptures of comfort for my weary soul. Knowing that God was holding me at the moment when I felt lonely brought me comfort. I noticed there was nothing there about vengeance on this person. What He did was, He took care of my broken-heart and reassured me of His love. I found enough comfort to fall asleep peacefully that night.

If that were the end, then there would be no need for this book. But I am writing because many, who are reading this, are in similar position as I was, though the situation may differ. There are those who are still stinging from past hurts and abuse, others are still clinging to grudges, and pain from their childhood. Many are still literally having nightmares from traumatic experiences; some are walking lonely friendless path, overwhelmed by shame, distraught and traumatized. Unforgiveness, breeding resentment, bitterness and self-hatred have crushed the heart of many, causing them to live questionable lifestyles. All these carry the burden of unforgiveness from place to place.

We might think it is okay to hold the thought of the offence in our heart because someone did something to me or against me, but nothing could be further from the truth; I thought I had the right to be mad, to hold that person hostage in unforgiveness! But that is not God's best and I wanted His best for my life. I realized I am no different from any other but God allowed me the privilege of going through that experience, and may I say many after that, to teach me a valuable lesson on forgiveness.

Yes! Forgiveness! It's the word no one wants to hear, especially when an injustice or an injury have been committed. Many times, we would rather see that person or persons suffer as much pain as he or she had inflicted in our lives. That is the tendency of the human heart. We somehow feel that would make us feel better. That is how the enemy wants us to think and to live because he does not want us free and whole. He wants us to live a life of unforgiveness that is filled with unhappiness and misery. Jesus, however, does not want us living this way, thus he came to show us a better way. He showed me!

As I was driving to work one night, I worked the 11pm to 7am shift, at the hospital at the time, I heard so clearly the Holy Spirit as He began to unfold to me the story of the suffering and anguish that Jesus Christ endured at the hands of cruel men. I had known the passion story since childhood, but this was different. I was having a one on one encounter in my car, on my way to work, just like that. It was surreal what I was experiencing, but it's as if I was taken back in time to the scene of what happened over two thousand years ago. Never have I experienced such vision; not of things about to happen, but what had already happened.

In my mind's eye I "saw" the betrayal of Judas, one of Jesus' followers who walked with Him for three years, the denial of Peter who promised to defend him even to his own death. There Jesus stood, rejected, brokenhearted and alone; all the people who now turned their backs on Him, were the very ones He did nothing but good. He was beaten, spat upon, bruised and bleeding from the many whippings He received. He was left alone to face the unfair trials by the Sanhedrin Council. They placed a crown of thorns on His head; they mocked, jeered and ridiculed the Son of God. Finally, He the innocent one was hanged on a cross. Blood oozing from his wounds, but it was at that moment, at that time, when the pain was unbearable, He cried out, "Father, forgive them; for they know not what they do!" (Luke 23:34).

He, Jesus! The guiltless one, accused, beaten and crucified for nothing He had done. His only guilt was His love for mankind. After all that man had done, Jesus chose forgiveness over hatred. What amazed me though was that His forgiveness was instantaneous; it was not an afterthought. It was not after He came back in His glorified body, but rather when He could still feel the hurt in His body, hear their taunting. While He was still hanging on the wooden cross, in pain and barely breathing, as the sins of mankind were being transferred onto Him, right then at that moment, He chose to forgive.

The magnitude of what was revealed, captured my thought and like hot lava stones burned deep in my heart, totally transforming my life from that day forward. I considered the hurt of my own heart, and in light of what I "saw' and "heard" I realized how selfish I was in wanting justice for my accuser, instead of mercy and forgiveness. Oh how my cold heart melted, driving on that road to work that night. I made a very conscious decision right then and there. I CHOSE to forgive my accuser completely, from the heart! It was no longer about me, or my hurt. It was about releasing the person from the prison of my heart. After all, it was nothing compared to what Jesus suffered for me. I was focusing on me! In my eyes, I became my own idol. I had made a lovely bed, spread with satin sheets, for unforgiveness to reside in my heart. I did not want to let go of the wrong that was done. I was the victim! So I rehearsed it over and over continuing to make myself the victim instead of the victor.

God got my attention! I asked His forgiveness for my part in holding the person hostage in my heart and placing them on the throne of my heart where He belonged. I asked Him to heal my hurting heart from the pains that I have caused to reside there. I prayed also for my accuser right then. I realized then and there that I might never hear the words I previously wanted to hear, "Please forgive me," from the accuser, and I never did! But it did not matter anymore; I was set free and continue to live free.

Until you have made that decision, as I did years ago, you might not understand what I am about to say; but a transaction took place on that night, which I will never forget. I experienced the supernatural peace, which indeed surpassed all human understanding. God's presence was ever so real. I felt clean and more so FREE! He freed me from oppressing thoughts, He freed me from self-pity; I was free from the past! He freed me to love that person; I was set free! I was given a vivid picture of what true wholehearted forgiveness looks like. It was then, ever so gently, I heard the following: "Daughter, Forgiveness Is Not An Option!" There is no way around the act of forgiveness, but to forgive from the heart.

My prayer is that as you read this book you will begin to experience God's unconditional love flowing through you. He loves us so much He gave Heaven's best, His only Begotten son, to come into the world to show us His best for our lives. He showed me! Now by His help, I will share the blessing by which He has blessed me in learning to forgive others as He forgave us. I will not dare to say I have not been hurt since, nor can I say I have not unintentionally hurt others, but I can truly say forgiving others is by far better for me, because of the object lesson that was revealed to me of Jesus' act of forgiveness. If He can forgive me of the many sins I have either committed and or omitted, then I can forgive those who have trespassed against me. I need His forgiveness, do you?

Chapter 1

"The weak can never forgive. Forgiveness is the attribute of the strong."
Mahatma Gandhi

Understanding Forgiveness

In understanding forgiveness and the power that emanates from the forgiver, should give us a better perspective on releasing forgiveness to others often and quickly. Forgiveness truly demands a strong mindset and a willingness to be vulnerable. It moves us beyond our comfort zone and into uncharted territory. Most find it much easier to keep the grudge going than to forgive. When forgiveness is released, however, it caused the weak to become strong and gives the offended authority to claim back his or her life that was hijacked by the wrong doer.

When we continue to stay in that vegetated state of unforgiveness, it gives the enemy power to control our lives. He does that by allowing the memory of the offence to linger in our thoughts, almost on a daily basis, stirring within us deep emotions from what happened long ago. As the thoughts come alive, the situation is relived, the pain is rekindled and the cycle goes on. These persons will never find peace within themselves to live a fully productive and quality life.

As long as the pain is nurtured, then forgiveness will not be possible. That is, until there is a change in the mindset. This is why although forgiveness is a much written about topic; and is preached from millions of pulpits frequently yet, it has become a growing epidemic among born again believers, and the non-believers alike. Until the root of unforgiveness is extracted by the release of forgiveness, unforgiveness will continue to cause shattered homes and desolate lives; as is evident by the increasing number of no-fault divorces, abuse and many losses of lives.

Many individuals continue to hold on to grudges and past hurts that were never resolved from generations past. There are mothers who are at odds with their daughters and likewise, daughters who are having difficulty forgiving mothers from things said or done in childhood. So also are fathers and sons, wives and husbands, sisters and brothers and the list goes on. Consequently, the chance of this behavior being perpetrated in future generations is inevitable. Unforgiveness could be passed from generation to generation without anyone knowing why the feud, who started it or when and where it started.

Generational Conflicts and Curses

Sometime ago, my business took me to a small town, in the state where I live. While there, I heard the most interesting story of a long standing feud between two neighboring cities that had been fighting among themselves for decades, much like the Hatfields and McCoys in West Virginia-Kentucky in the late nineteenth century. It was told to me that countless life had been lost, relationships severed and families ruined because of this feud. Naturally, I then asked what the feud was about and what provoked it. I was promptly told, "I don't know." I again asked about the origin or the history of the feud, who or what started it, but the response was the same. The person relating this to me, who was middle age, could not tell me how it started, who started it or why.

The story told to me was that it started before many of the locals were born. As a matter of fact, many were born into that situation and it involved families. Although, it is somewhat better than before, the rivalry still continues and it does not take much to set the 'fire' of unforgiveness to blaze again at the drop of a hat. This feud, started long before much of the citizens fifty and below were born, has now become generational. Why is it continuing? Because no one is willing to repent for the past sin, ask forgiveness of each other and move on into a brighter future of love and peace.

Unforgiveness has touched many lives and has eaten away at the very fabric of our society. Each of us can say that at one time or another, we have encountered someone struggling with this issue of unforgiveness. Maybe, even as you are reading this, there is evidence of unforgiveness in your own heart towards someone who has done you wrong, and your intention is to sever the relationship and not have anything to do with such person again. It is not a coincidence that you are holding this book in your hand? God wants you healed, delivered and set free! He wants you to live life abundantly with joy and peace through the power of forgiveness. You owe it to yourself to live from your strength and not your weakness. Even more importantly, you do not want to pass on this 'legacy' of unforgiveness into the next generation.

The Killer of Forgiveness

There are subtle agents that can suffocate or kill forgiveness in its embryonic stage and must be avoided at all cost. I stated in the introduction that I chose not to bring any other person in on what I was going through. At that time, I did not fully understand it, but in looking back I realized that was a divine plan from above, and not of me. A wrong counsel can set you back degrees in the forgiveness process. You might believe you are being helped but instead, find yourself getting deeper into unforgiveness because instead of going forward you are now moving backwards.

As the wrong deed is being rehearsed, over and over, you become comforted with the fact that the person does not deserve your forgiveness. The "counselor," empathized and sympathize with us because they, "understanding" what you are going through. They identify themselves with your problem. Often they have stories of their own disgorging from their lips; their hearts ooze negativity and unforgiveness. Together an altar is now erected to the "god of unforgiveness." Often they would go there to "worship" their pain and hurts. No healing will ever take place in this environment. When there is constant rehearsal of the situation it does nothing but pour fuel on the unforgiving heart causing it to blaze and forgiveness is stifled and or suffocated. Positive reinforcement is needed to help you gain back control of your already broken life. It is wise to choose well the person you call advisor or counselor, as their influence in your life will either build you or break you down.

If your counselor still has issues of his or her own, then you might need to find someone else to advise or counsel you because the damage can be greater if bad advice is given. When we surround ourselves with people who are honest and positive in character they will remind us of the freedom that comes from releasing forgiveness to the offender. Such persons should have the ability to share with you their own 'war' stories of past experiences but also how they triumphed. This would give one hope and a way forward, towards forgiving and releasing of the hurt they have allowed to grow in the heart. Hurting people hurt others. Therefore it will take a healthy heart to heal a hurting one.

The Principles of Forgiveness
Looking at the definition for forgiveness, according to Collins Gem Dictionary, to forgive is to "cease to blame or hold resentment against; to pardon." In the Thesaurus the synonyms of forgive are: "acquit," "absolve," "exonerate," "excuse." [1] I am sure we have heard these words in legal court cases where

someone is acquitted or pardoned of some act for which they were on trial.

Many of us can still remember the O.J. Simpson trial of 1994, when he was accused of killing his ex-wife, Nicole, and her friend, Ron Goldman. It could have been dubbed, 'the trial of the century.' Many believed he was guilty, while others believed otherwise. It was up to the jury, however, to decide his innocence or his guilt based upon evidence received at the trial. He went to trial for the double murder but was later found "not guilty!" He was totally exonerated by the judicial system. Many were angry about the verdict, while others cheered, but a jury of his peers, based on evidence presented, found him not guilty. He was free, released from prison and was back in society as if nothing happened.

This is an example of what the forgiveness looks like from the earthly judicial system; but it mimics what forgiveness looks like from Heaven's Supreme Court, when we cease to hold grudge against any. Nicole and Ron were both dead, their families hurting, but the person they presumed did the killing was set free. You might say where is the justice in this? Now let's argue that O.J. supposedly did the act he was accused of, how could he walk free? Actually some people are still up in arms about whether he is guilty or not.

Well, let us look at the definition again. It did not say a person is not guilty, rather it said, "Cease to blame or hold resentment against; to pardon." When one is freed, exonerated or pardoned it means just that, they cannot again be tried for the crime from which they were acquitted. Meaning whether a person is guilty of a crime or not, once the verdict is issued it becomes final. So too, when we from our hearts, have forgiven someone of their trespass, by the above definition it has becomes final. There is nothing left to do.

Earlier in my marriage my husband and I made a pact that once an issue we disagreed on was fully discussed and settled, we would never bring that issue to life again; nor would we go to bed angry at each other. That means that whatever needs to be said should be said and forgiveness is asked and we move on. Well, there was a time when that was not enough for me. Although apologies were made, I was still fuming! "He cannot just ask forgiveness and walk away," I thought. So I kept it going.

Finally, my hubby looked me in the eyes and said these words I have never forgotten these many years; "Honey," he said, "I have asked your forgiveness already, what else can I do? If there is something else please tell me." Somehow those humble words hit me so hard and reverberated in my head. Indeed! What else was there for him to do? What else? It was up to me to receive his forgiveness and set my own heart free. He was free, but I was locked in my own prison of unforgiveness. He however, had moved on with his life. He had offered his apology to him it was final. I was still stuck in the old mindset of the past. Forgiveness is the end of all matter, when it is done conscientiously from the heart.

Forgiveness means putting that situation to rest, not regurgitating and bringing it back to life at will. Just as Jesus' act on Calvary was final, complete. He never reminds us of our acts of iniquity against Him. He has totally forgiven us of our transgressions, though they were many. It is done away with gone forever! We are pardoned and made free! Guilt should no longer be a factor in our lives because we are pardoned. Our response is to accept that truth and continue to live a life transformed by the grace of God.

The Act Pardon

Often when a president is leaving office, he would perform an act of goodwill by pardoning someone who has done or was guilty of committing a crime. It would be totally up to the discretion of the president as to whom he would pardon. The pardon is not to say that the person was not guilty but rather it is saying, "You are guilty, but now you have been given a second chance to live a better life through the power of that pardon." It would be up to that person to receive that act of goodwill or to stay locked up because of the overridden conscience of guilt.

Forgiveness is an act of goodwill to those who have offended, physically hurt, abused, damaged or tarnished someone's reputation, or any other ill will you can think of. Forgiveness must be extended to everyone. We struggle with forgiveness because it is hard to comprehend forgiving someone who has done such heinous injustice to humanity, would be forgiven. This is why the forgiver has to have a renewed mindset. It will not be easy, but it is something that must be done to set us free. Now, when we release forgiveness to the offender, it's up to him or her to receive it, but whether they receive it or not, we are free to move on with our life. Unfortunately, there are many still locked away in their own prison not understanding that pardon has been granted, and he or she is now free to live again.

The verb "forgive" is recorded over fifty-three times throughout the Bible. Jesus, Himself, taught on the fundamental topic of forgiveness, on numerous occasions. As a matter of fact, at the lowest point in His earthly life, while hanging on the cross, He cried out "Father, forgive them; for they know not what they do." (Luke 23:34) Jesus in this selfless act, while in deep agony, showed us what true forgiveness looks like. It was conscious, uncalculating and instantaneous. He is the God who leads by example. He will not ask us to do anything that He first has not done. He has left us the legacy in forgiveness. Not only that but He has endowed us with His strength, which He said, "Is made perfect in our weakness;" enabling us to forgive everyone, no matter who it is that has hurt us.

Let me go further in reminding us that all of us were guilty of sinning against God. According to the Word of God, we were all born in sin; none is exempt from that statement. We all were at one time, or still are guilty of trespassing against the Creator. God sent His only Son into the world to acquit, absolve, and exonerate everyone who will accept Him as Lord and Savior. We are made free by Him as if nothing happened. We are free, pardoned! We were guilty as charged but through Christ's blood we are now made free from all acts of unrighteousness against God. Because we are of a sinful nature we will continue to need His forgiveness, He is the only perfect one; but when forgiveness is given the offence is done away with forever.

Forgiveness is a conscious decision that must be made by the offended (the one who is affronted). In Jesus' teachings on forgiveness, He asserted to His hearers a statement that I believe cuts across the grain. This is what He said, "If you know that the brother ought against you, you are to leave your gifts at the altar and go reconcile with him." Italics meant to stress the point. It is not the offender who is called into question here but rather the person who was offended. This statement might have stirred a reaction in the hearts of His listeners; His close disciples too, must have gone silent on Jesus as they listened in stupefaction to this teaching.

After all this is something new. Shouldn't the one who did the offense be responsible for their action and come to ask for pardon? Agreeably so, but Jesus was now releasing the responsibility of freedom on the offended person. In other words, if the hurt person's freedom depends solely on waiting for the wrongdoer to apologize, then that might not happen. It did not happen for me, I never received an apology either but in forgiving the person I was made free. Jesus knew that for the person to walk in true freedom, he or she must first be released from the bondage within. We are told to "leave our gifts there in front of the altar. First go and be reconciled to the person; then come and offer your gift." (Matthew 5:24) So the acceptance of your gift depends on you releasing forgiveness to your offender.

Forgiveness and Reconciliation

Often times we confuse forgiveness or pardoning someone with reconciling with the person; but these are two different things. While in pardon we offer forgiveness and mercy, reconciliation on the other hand means: "reunion, or bringing together again." While we must offer pardon, it does not necessarily mean that the relationship will return to the original state.

Unfortunately, sometimes that cannot happen because of the severity or the breach in that relationship. For instance, if it was a child molestation issue, then for sure there can be forgiveness, but reconciliation might not be possible especially where the law is concerned. A Woman, who is constantly living in fear of her life, because of spousal abuse or any other situations or circumstances in like manner, might not find reconciliation possible. What forgiveness does mean is that the offended person would have set him or herself free, from that burden of unforgiveness.

In a less severe case, if reconciliation is at all possible then do so with proper guidelines. Do not, in your haste to reconcile, allow yourself to be swept away into fallacy instead of recognizable truth. If apology was not done and issues worked out, then chances are nothing will change. This is why professional counseling might be necessary for your healing first, before any consideration of reconciliation. When you are healed from the situation that you were in or from what was done to you, only then will you have a clearer mind to look at the situation from a different perspective. When our emotion is besieged by painful experiences, we become vulnerable to anything, even untruth; therefore, you will need time for healing. One way to help in the healing process is to feed your spirit with positive reinforcements that come through the reading of Scriptures as well as good wise counsel.

The reason why forgiveness must be given even if reconciliation is not possible is, while we are waiting for the offender to ask forgiveness, several changes are taking place in the heart. The heart has now become a combat zone for malice, anger, resentment and murderous thoughts to reside. The one who was offended, has to keep that malice of the offense constantly in the forefront of his or her mind at all times; meanwhile the heart is being moved farther away from the peace and security that is found only in Christ. We no longer experience true joy because our thoughts are filled with revenge as we wallow in self-pity and anger and rage. We have allowed that blot of unforgiveness to become both mountainous and an anchor in our lives.

Jesus did not relinquish the responsibility of our souls to the wrongdoer. That responsibility He has left to us. We cannot be answerable for the actions of others, but we must take responsibility for our response to the actions of others. He therefore, exhorts us to forgive and live a life of freedom. In other words, first free your own heart from the entanglements within. The offender has a responsibility, but in truth, we are responsible for what goes in and out of our own heart. Again, pardoning someone might not necessarily mean reconciliation is possible; but in pardoning others you have submit your soul to God, and this is true liberty.

Chapter 2

"Forgiveness is the fragrance that the violet sheds on the heel that has crushed it."
Mark Twain

Misnomers about Forgiveness

Not forgiving someone who has hurt you can become a selfish matter of the heart. This sounds like a very strong statement but really the truth is, if in forgiving we liberate ourselves from the offense and dislodge the offender from our heart, then we should seek to do so, at all cost. In holding on to this hurtful experience, and by keeping the memory alive, is quite damaging to you and your wellbeing. The constant rehearsing of it to yourself or to those, whom you come in contact, or even crying in silence, is hurting you! Not the offender.

Although an injustice was done that initiated injury to your life, when it all plays out, it becomes more about you accepting or not accepting that injury to control your life. If you find yourself constantly repeating, "I am the one who is hurting or no one knows what I am going through," or "poor me," then possibly you have accepted the role of being a victim without the power to initiate change to your life.

At this juncture, the matter becomes more about "me and my hurts," instead of availing yourself to get the necessary help to assist you to live a productive life beyond the offense, and start a new chapter. You were created with a purpose in mind; therefore, do not allow your destiny to be hijacked by anyone. Consider the situation as a blip on your radar to detour you from greater things. The longer your stay in that "crippled" position the longer it will take to get to your appointed destiny.

Think about it! You did not bring that situation unto yourself, but even if you feel that you did, it is time to recover and rediscover your purpose. Get the necessary help you need to get past the unsavory experience. You should be ready to alleviate yourself of the burden you carry. By no means should it be worn like a trophy. In doing so you are now holding the offender captive in your heart and you have now become a prisoner in your own penitentiary. It is very wise to examine the heart to know what captivates it the most. As you discover inconsistencies, take action immediately. Do not allow malice or any other thing to fester.

Heart Trouble

The heart is the seat of all imaginations. It is the heart that prompts our attitude and actions. It contrives, rehearses and executes the action plan of the thing it devises. It will not readily pardon or let go of the situation until positive reinforcement is installed. Only then will the bad things be deleted. The Scripture speaks of the heart, in Jeremiah 17:9, "The human heart is the most deceitful of all things, and desperately wicked. Who really know how bad it is?" Whatever is contrived in the heart prompts our behavior. This is true in every case, whether it is the joy of the Lord we are experiencing, or evil thoughts or ideologies, it does not matter, they will eventually be manifested outwardly.

I find that, irrespective of all the religious things we do, an unforgiving heart cannot truly find lasting peace. Religion will medicate but not heal! We sometimes bury the truth of forgiveness beneath religious experiences or over-medicating ourselves with everything but the necessary food of the Word. The truth is, however, there is no shortcut to finding true, lasting peace without forgiving our adversaries. When this peace is found, then we can begin to enter into loving intimate relationship with the Lord.

To experience such relationship with God, our hearts must be fully opened for His inspection. True fellowship requires that we expose our heart to the Lord and in so doing all the hidden matters of the heart will be revealed. Once we allow Him to examine our hearts and motives all that have been concealed within, and which have obstructed, our fellowship with Him will now be made known. This revelation is not to bring sorrow but one that calls us to repentance. As we humble ourselves to Him and ask His forgiveness then true healing will begin. This is the beginning of a triumphant victory over the past.

We will no longer be satisfied with struggling to be happy; instead we will be experiencing lasting joy. Joy comes at the point of our yielding to the Lord and Him endowing us with fresh supply of grace. When our heart is truly healed, our eyes are removed from our person, and our circumstances, and we now begin to look differently at things on a whole. God's divine plan for our lives will begin to unfold. No longer will the future seems so dismal but new life begins to spring forth. When forgiveness is done from the heart, joy will replace resentments, bitterness, unhealthy thoughts and self-pity.

Ultimate Joy

Joy is lasting or abiding and does not depend on circumstances or situations to be. Happiness on the other hand is temporary. For instance we are happy when we receive a raise in our paycheck or a change in position, etc.; but soon, we are unhappy about the very thing we were once happy about. Happiness goes but so far but joy is constant. God wants us to experience undiluted joy. Psalm 16:11 says, "You make known to me the path of life; in your presence there is fullness of joy; at your right hand are pleasures forevermore." God not only wants us to experience joy but 'fullness of joy,' or ultimate joy. You can experience that joy today! Don't be short-changed by the enemy's lies. Be a good steward over your heart and win the battle of unforgiveness to gain that lasting joy and peace.

The enemy will keep us living half-truths, instead of the whole-truth of the Father's love towards us until we declare, "Enough is enough!" Refuse to believe that the devil is keeping you from forgiving others, because that is not all truth. The truth is, he only uses what is given to him. He is neither omniscience or omnipresent. He does not know nor can he read our minds. He uses familiar spirits to do his work. What we display in our behavior to others or what comes from our mouths, determines what the adversary will use against us to keep us in bondage. You have the authority to change that.

The doorknob to a new life can only be opened from the inside; that is by you. You have the power in you to fight your way into freedom. Again, do not allow yourself to become crippled and useless by the past. You are able to overcome the very thing that caused you such pain. Begin to renounce unforgiveness from your heart and then let the joy of the Lord fill you daily. By doing this you will find peace with yourself and others. The choice is yours...the reward is great.

Chapter 3

"He who cannot forgive breaks the bridge over which he himself must pass."
George Herbert

Reasons for Unforgiveness

We hold on to unforgiveness for many reasons; too many. The enemy is the master deceiver and schemer and has been instrumental in bringing about heartaches, hurts and pain. Jesus warned us in John 10 that the devil is a thief and a liar; there is nothing good in him, so we are not denying his part in what was done. We, however, must not give him the pleasure of using us in continuing to carry out his hateful schemes. His duty is to destroy those who belong to the Lord, and ruin our relationship with God and others. He will stop at no length in keeping us from doing what is right. He knows that in doing wrong things it empowers him and gives him prominence in your life. He is attracted to chaos.

When I was much younger, I would often hear my mother say, "If you give the devil an inch, he will eventually take the entire measuring stick." That's how he works and will continue to work. He is not contented with inflicting pain, his whole aim is to destroy your life by whatever means necessary. He is well aware that when he hurts you he is hurting the apple of God's eye. You are very precious to the heart of the Father. Your welfare is irrevocable in God's hand.

God has a plan for your life! But unfortunately the devil does too. God's plan is to prosper you, to give you hope and a

---

future, Jeremiah. 29:11. On the other hand, the enemy's plan is to destroy you, even in the embryonic stage of your life so that you will not realize your potential. In other words, he short-circuits your destiny and robs you of the joy and peace that could have been yours through Christ.

There necessarily must be resistance, on your part, in not giving him right of entry to your life. This can be done when we acknowledge any open door to our heart, and take responsibility over your own heart. As long as unforgiveness is present, he has access into your life...legal grounds, if you will, to do as it pleases him. Unforgiveness is an open door or path into your life. In the book of James, we are exhorted to "resist the devil and he will flee," James 4:7. Give him no place by hording unforgiveness in your heart. Take control and take that which belongs to God.

You must claim heaven's diplomatic immunity, which is, to run into the Embassy of God's divine grace where He will give you all the protection necessary, to avoid harassment from the evil one. He can do that because we are of God's Kingdom, we are accepted because of His well beloved son. Refuse to live with the excuse of helplessness. That is the devil's lie. You are not helpless you have providence on your side, by your side and residing in you. Turn the situation over to Him, and allow the healing to begin.

Forgiving and Forgetting
Other reasons why we might find it hard to forgive could be because we infringe forgiveness on forgetting the wrong that was done by the offender. We will never forget unless permanent amnesia is involved. Memories are lasting pictures of the mind. Let's face it, we are human, created by a loving God with the capacity to think, to feel, to love, to enjoy life and share memories, whether they are good or bad.

Many have stockpiled memories, from early childhood, of things they have done and would like to erase them, if it were at all possible. Memories however, are snapshots of the past. Each day a new snapshot is taken and a memory is created whether good or bad. Unfortunately, the mind cannot filter the bad and leave the good, it does not work that way, and so memories are created and remain and will continue to be stored in the mind as long as we live. Memories are just what they are memories, for better or for worse. They are there not to haunt or to cause pain, but rather they are examples by which we grow and live.

Because of those stored memories from the past we sometimes find it hard to forgive ourselves, but in order to forgive others, you must first practice the gift of forgiveness to yourself. Childish memories from the past, which you are still having difficulty forgiving yourself, should remain in the past. We should not allow the ghost of yesterday to inflict punishment on the present and thus injuring the future. No one can turn the hand of time backwards therefore; it's good that one should settle the actuality of self-forgiveness first. In so doing this would open the heart to forgive others. If you cannot forgive yourself, you will have difficulty forgiving others.

We can agree that forgiveness is not based on forgetting, but the attitude by which one remembers the act is what is brought into question here. Forgiving the wrongdoer does not mean that one will instantly forget the offence. What it does mean though is that we will no longer endure the constant pain of the experience. As we release forgiveness over the situation, over time our mind seems to lose its ability to recall the incident and bitter details any longer. In other words, if and when you bring to mind the incident it would be void of the anger and bitterness and resentment once felt.

The Amish Story

In the process of writing this book, I saw, for the first time a drama titled *Amish Grace*, a Lifetime movie based on a true story that was debuted, March 28, 2010. [2] As I watched this epic story of a senseless shooting that took place in the community of Nickel Mines, Pennsylvania, I watched the most mind boggling story of forgiveness I could ever behold. Here I was seeing this Lifetime movie, almost four years after the film's debut, but how apropos.

This is the story of a community devastated by the irrational schoolhouse shooting of five beautiful Amish girls, leaving their parents in deep grief and having to bury their children. The gunman, who was living in the same community, also left behind a wife and young children. One of the dead girl's father and the elders of the Amish community went to visit the wife of the shooter to let her know that they had forgiven her husband for taking the lives of their children. "We will not allow hatred into our hearts. We know that you will be experiencing some harsh judgments, and we would like to offer our help. We are your neighbors, and if you and your children should need anything we hope you would let us know."

It was shocking not only to the shooter's wife, but to the news media and onlookers from within as well as from outside of the community, that they would so readily forgave the person who did such a horrific crime, on the very day of the killings. How foolish forgiveness seems to those who do not understand the principles of it. The elders of the community did exactly what Jesus did on the cross. While he was still hanging there bruised and hurting, He forgave mankind of their sins. One of the elders from the Amish community said, "Forgiveness comes from an open heart or it is not forgiveness at all." How true that is! A heart that is not open cannot give or receive forgiveness.

So many thought provoking nuggets on forgiveness were spoken in that film that remains as food for the spirit. Speaking from his pain, one of the fathers said, "Forgiveness does not mean forgetting." No it does not! But it does mean that daily we strive to release the memory of the pain to God. Only He, in time will cause the pain to diminish and memory to be healed. A mother of one of the girls who was killed said that she has to offer her anger to God, and then in another hour she has to do it all over again and again.

The memory we will live with. The loss of those girls left a void that only time can heal. The memory of what happened on that fateful day will live on with the parents, families and friends forever, but forgiveness was already issued to the wife of the killer, it is up to her to receive it.

The situation I encountered years ago is still a part of my memory. As a matter of fact, I have shared my story as a testimony of God's healing power, on several occasions without injuring the person in anyway. The difference is however, there is no bitterness or pain attached to the memory as it was prior to me releasing forgiveness. I have seen the person on several occasions and I am no longer affected by the past, because healing was accomplished through the release of forgiveness to the person. To release unforgiveness from your heart is like extracting poison from something, thus causing that thing to become acceptable or pure again.

Seeking Divine Intervention

Just as cancer grows from one bad cell and infiltrates organs and tissues over a period of time, so too unforgiveness like cancer, if left untreated, eats away at the very core of our relationship both with man and with God. Just as cancer needs radical medical intervention to destroy its infestation and to prolong the life of the patient; so too, in like manner, must unforgiveness be dealt with radically, through the power of forgiveness, to stop its infestation in our lives.

The person who is sick with the cancer however, would seek for the best Oncologist, whom he or she believes would give him or her the very best chance of survival. Likewise, the offended person who has unforgiveness in his or her heart must seek out the best Heart Specialist, who in this case, is Christ Jesus. Medical science cannot do this. He created the heart and He knows all about it. He will remove from your heart that 'lump' of unforgiveness that it will no longer destroy your flow of joy and peace. He will not leave you alone post-surgery either. He promised that he would be with you always. For every tinge of pain you will experience in the future, He will be there to bring you comfort and love. He awaits your call.

Now you must not allow the enemy to enslave you any longer and weigh you down with the baggage of unforgiveness. No one likes to be looked on or be treated as a slave. Slavery means you have no freedom to do as you please. You are under the burden of the person who dictates to you what to do. When we hold unforgiveness in our hearts we have given that person 'master control' over our lives. You are truly never free from the oppressive thoughts of that person. Each thought comes with a reaction of some sorts, whether bitterness or resentment or anger, you are never free!

The person who did the wrong, on the other has moved on; possible hurting others or they might have gone on to a life of repentance. In the meantime, the one who was offended still continues to hold on to the hurts and pain. He or she has not left the place where the incident happened. As long as you continue in this unforgiving state you will forever remain stagnant. When you forgive the person, however, you free yourself from his or her control over our life and disgorged them from your heart. You are liberated to live again. You will be able to breathe the fresh air of freedom from the tyranny of the past. You are free to live life abundantly. You will now have the authority to help set others as you are. Seek to live free!

Chapter 4

"And forgive us our debts, as we also have forgiven our debtors" –
Matthew 6: 12

The Kingdom Principle: Forgiveness

If I could ask a question of you, "How many times do you believe you have done some wrong to another person? Can you count? No!" In reality we cannot count from childhood until now, or even in our adult years, how many times we have used the phrase, "I am sorry, please forgive me," and expect that that person would indeed forgive us as we asked. How incredible it is, that when we are offended, by another person we find it so hard to forgive him or her? Why is that so? Isn't it equally important for that person to experience the forgiveness you receive from one you have done wrong?

Unforgiveness is an age-old problem. It was no different in Jesus' time either. Peter came to Jesus and asked of him, "Lord, how often shall my brother sin against me, and I forgive him? Till seven times?" (Matthew 18:23-3) His reply? "I say not unto you, until seven times: but, until seventy times seven." Peter could only perceive seven times. After all, that is the perfect number isn't it? Moreover, the rabbinical teaching said to forgive three times. He went up four above the rabbinical teachings. He thought he would have scored brownie points with Jesus for his answer. Instead he hears what? I can just imagine the incredulous look on Peter's face. He must have been thinking, "Lord are you crazy? Do you understand the math? You are talking about 490 times! In what? A day, a month, a year, or a lifetime" "Did you not understand the question Jesus?"

Oh, don't shake your head at Peter. How many times God has spoken a word to us and we ask something like "Are you sure Lord? That's a lot of money to give or that's a far journey to go visit that person..."

While Peter was trying to pick his face off the floor, Jesus continued with a story about a king who was reviewing his business and found a servant who owed him much money, ten thousand talents to be exact. I am by no means a math major, but in researching the equivalence to our currency today, it would amount to over a million dollars. The servant could not pay that sum back to the lord. The lord ordered him to be sold along with his wife and children and his possessions so he could reclaim some of his money.

On hearing this, the servant fell down and worshiped him and begged for mercy until he could pay his debt. Being moved with compassion, the lord forgave him of his debt and set him free. That very servant, that was showed forgiveness, found a fellow servant as himself who owed him only a few dollars. He grabbed him by the throat and demanded that he paid back all that he owed him. The fellow servant pleaded with him for mercy, but he gave him none. Instead, he had him thrown into prison, until he could pay the debt.

The lord, who had forgiven the servant, heard about what the unforgiving servant did, he summoned him and said to him, "O thou wicked servant, I forgave you all that debt because thou asked of me. Should you not also have compassion on thy fellow servant, even as I had pity on you?" With that he delivered him to the tormentors until he could pay his debt to the lord.

Peter must have been slowly shaking his head from side to side in awe as Jesus again declares, "So likewise shall my heavenly Father do also unto you, if you from your hearts forgive not everyone his brother their trespasses." Those words must have been like a hammer driving nails in a coffin. He was hearing this rendition from Jesus, the Master Teacher Himself! The Rabbi! What was Jesus doing? Jesus was teaching His disciples a lesson in Kingdom dynamics, which goes beyond what they had ever heard before. Jesus took forgiveness from religious platitudes to a higher level of Kingdom living.

Seven for Peter might have been a good number, he could fathom that; he could keep score at least; but Jesus' 70 x 7 = 490 times were not meant to be counted literally. The principle Jesus was teaching his disciples was: forgiveness is indefinite. It is not a onetime happening. It is over the period of a lifetime therefore, we cannot put a number to it, just as He does not put a limit to the number of times he has forgiven us of our trespasses against the Him.

What Jesus really was telling his disciples, and everyone within hearing was that we should live a life of forgiveness; it is a lifestyle that must be lived out daily. Why? Because we are going to slip up one-way or another, and will need each other's forgiveness! Jesus' teachings were designed to take us into a higher sphere of Kingdom living. There is no middle ground in this Kingdom. Its principles must be adhered to and lived out in fullness.

We often miss this teaching on Kingdom dynamics and have used it in an isolated manner. But everything Jesus did and taught was about the Kingdom of God! He was conveying the message of the Kingdom that He declared has come! He is the ultimate fulfillment of the Kingdom. Thus if His disciples were to enter the Kingdom, not just seeing it from afar, there must be a denial of oneself; in order to embrace and be devoted to the Kingdom and all that it stands for. Jesus walked out on earth what is lived in Heaven. He gave us the principles of the Kingdom that we might know how to live on earth.

Jesus' use of the parables in His teachings was specific, in that they point us to the Kingdom and its operations. It was designed to bring revelation to its citizen of what the Kingdom of Heaven is about, and how in understanding the message we must apply the teachings to our lives. When His Kingdom operation is continually before our eyes, and foremost in our hearts, then our walk will become more like Him. As Sovereign in the Kingdom of Heaven, He has offered forgiveness to all who will receive it. The citizen should follow in like example. As we focus on His teachings, we are being changed from glory to glory into His image and unforgiveness cannot take residence in our hearts.

Unforgiveness is a sin as much as covetousness, lying, adultery or any other conceivable sin. While each one can separate us from Christ, the truth is that we will confess some of the above mentioned sins but it seems like somehow unforgiveness goes un-repented than most. Repentance however, is the necessary ingredient, not only to enter into the Kingdom, but to living and enjoy the benefits therein. It is imperative that we identify the things that are toxic to our life and readily renounce them, in order to inherit eternal life.

Each person should purpose in his or her heart to do a daily Kingdom check-up, to see how healthy he or she is in his or her personal walk with the Lord. Is there any 'fever' of anger? Any "chill" of malice? Any "pain" of unforgiveness? Any "aching" from lovelessness? Is there any spiritual apathy about the sins in our lives? This is a good time as any to purge these sins from our lives and embrace Kingdom of God. We must actively participate in renouncing unforgiveness from our lives at all cost. Remember, we will need forgiveness; therefore, we must be willing likewise to forgive those who have trespassed against us. As the Father loves us so we also must show love to our fellowman. These are the principles of the Kingdom in which we have become a citizen.

Chapter 5

"Love recognizes no barriers. It jumps hurdles, leaps fences, penetrates walls to arrive at its destination full of hope."
Maya Angelou

Kingdom Principle – Unconditional Love

Unforgiveness reveals a love problem in our lives. "What does love have to do with forgiveness?" one might ask, the answer is "everything!" The Kingdom of God was established by and is demonstrated in love. The Gospel of John 3:16, declares "For God so Loved the world, that He gave His only Begotten Son, that whosoever believes in him, should not perish but have everlasting life." There are two principles that govern the Kingdom of Heaven: Love the Lord with all your heart and love your neighbor as yourself.

The Kingdom of Heaven is about LOVE! God's love! No one is perfect; we were all born in sin. When one comes to know the Savior and is being transferred into this new life, we will find that love and forgiveness are the abundant ingredients in this Kingdom. Without God's love flowing through us forgiveness is deficient. Someone said, "You can forgive someone without loving, but you cannot love someone without forgiving." This saying remains true in every situation we will encounter. The Scripture says, "Love covers a multitude of sins."

Some time ago I was struggling with a situation that I never gave thought to as a love problem. Each time this thing would surface in my spirit, I would ask God to help me move on from that place. If I have forgiven I did not want to keep thinking about the problem any longer, but I couldn't get the release I needed. Let me pause here to say that God answers every prayer. He might not answer the way you envisioned, but He will answer based on what lesson He chose for you to grow by.

For me, it was the 1 Corinthians 13, the Love Chapter. I was impressed in my spirit to go to that particular chapter, while in my quiet time. As I read through the chapter, I felt the compulsion in my spirit to put my name everywhere the word love or charity was mentioned. As I did so, I began to see the mind of God through the revelation of His word. I got the message loud and clear. I could not truly say I was all that in love. What an eye opener! If I am to live the Kingdom life in fullness then love must be the mainstream or the outflow of everything I do. It was not to be partial or polluted, just as His love is impartial and pure. I had to make a conscious effort daily, in demonstrating love to all, just as Christ loves me. I had to grow in love and walk it out in my everyday life.

It is interesting to know that when God has a plan for your life it requires a different mindset. He allows us to go but so far on what knowledge we have, but in order to be elevated to the next level, then there must be a change in our thinking and our practices. A short-cut method will not do. Most of our lives have been lived that way, finding the quickest answer for everything possible. Nothing is wrong with that when time is of the essence. It should not, however, become the norm in our spiritual walk. If it does, we would miss the fundamental truth from lessons that we will garner from adhering to the principles of life.

Forgiveness to many is a process that must be walked through. Unfortunately, as stated earlier, there are no shortcuts to us obtaining victory in that area of our lives; we must walk it out. God is a God of miracles; He can do anything it pleases Him to do. If a miracle is needed, He can do that, but there are times when we just got to walk out our healing. It's call processing. How you handle the process will determine your altitude.

Needless to say, in understanding the absent ingredient was good for me. The experience made me understand the truth of what was hindering my behavior to move beyond that inactive place in my life. In adjusting my life according to the Word I found my life again. I needed to grow in true love, the Agape kind of love: the love that is unconditional. A quick-fixed approach was not the answer. That would only take me but so far, but in learning the truth of my own heart where love is concern had a lifetime impact. I had to go through the process. Each time that something springs up in my heart I now learn to judge the situation according to 1 Corinthians 13. If it's a love issue I know how to approach it. This truth has made me free forever.

Let me hasten to say that no miracle happened when I received that Scripture from the Lord. What it did however was to provoke me. It opened my eyes to understand that love was not operating in fullness in my life. We sometimes love but only so far. Having children has helped me to understand and developed the Agape love of God more than anything I know. We love our kids, no matter what they have done. We extend to them unconditional love, even when they don't deserve it. I have learned to appreciate God's unconditional love for me, through their eyes. Love is enduring and has a very long shelf life; it will never decay, never rust, never grows old and definitely will never come to an end. Everything else will terminate but love.

What is it that you need to walk out in your life? If you are a citizen of the Kingdom of God, He will not only reveal it to you but He will also give instructions to follow, if only you ask. Not only that, He will supply the grace necessary to help you through the process.

Love: What is it?

So what is LOVE! Is it a feeling? Is it a fact or fiction? So many books, preaching, teaching and now blogging, have been written or spoken about that endearing topic, "love," but what is it? How does a person, who was born with such sinful nature, and to whom hate comes more readily than love, now find him or herself accessing the divine love of Christ? I believe in order for the believer to function in love in the kingdom of God, he or she would have to seek to know God's love intimately. God knew that it would be very hard for frail humanity to understand this kind of love; so, as stated earlier, He sent Jesus Christ, His only Begotten Son, into the world to demonstrate what His love looks like, even to His death on the cross.

In researching the word "love" in the Old Testament I found two Hebrew words that I want to focus on. The first is "Ahava" which talks about the love between parents and a child, Genesis 22:2; or between close friends, as recorded between David and Jonathan, I Samuel 18:2; or between a man and a woman as seen in Songs of Solomon between the Bride and her Beloved.

The other word for love is "Chesed." According to Wikipedia, this love can be described as "loving-kindness" or "steadfast love" and has aspect of "affection and compassion." Daniel Elazar has suggested that "Chesed" cannot easily be translated into English, but that it means something like "loving covenant obligation," a kind of love that goes beyond a concern with compliance with following laws or contracts. [3]

In the New Testament, the word love, in the Greek language, speaks of "Eros" love as between a man and a woman; or "Phileo" as brotherly love or love of things; and the "Agape" love or selfless, unconditional, divine love. This love, the "Agape," is what the Kingdom of Heaven operates in. It's the God-kind of love. This love caused Jesus to lay aside the royalties of Heaven, His impeccable name and character to descend the earth, take the form of sinful man, suffers much shame and disgrace. He became a curse for us by hanging on the tree, so that we could be forgiven and set free.

This love is unselfish and kind. It puts the need of others above its own comfort. It seeks the welfare of others and is not easily provoked nor is it rude or boastful. No mankind from his flesh can invoke this Agape love. It is the gift of the Father to us, when first we received the free gift of salvation through Jesus Christ our Lord. He who is Love personified now comes to reside in our heart. Everything we do should reflect Him and His Kingdom. Unfortunately, because we were translated from another kingdom where darkness exists, we now must endeavor to come in alignment with all that this Kingdom offers.

In both "Chesed" in the Hebrew, and "Agape" in the Greek, you will notice they speak of loving kindness, steadfast and unconditional love. They are the love without limits or without boundaries. The words express both affection and compassion for others. These are the necessary ingredients needed to forgive those who have trespassed against us. Meaning that if we are short on Agape love in our daily walk, if we have not experienced that ourselves, then it will be quite difficult to forgive the person truly from our heart without any attachment. Both Chesed and Agape seek the welfare of others.

Agape does not consistently rehearse the wrong that was done. In other words, it does not take into account a wrong suffered neither does it rejoice in unrighteousness, it rejoices in the truth. 1 Corinthians 13:6. Agape recognizes that an injustice was done, but it does not revel in that fact, instead it seeks to bring an end to the wrong that was done.

Oh, no one could have felt more betrayed than Jesus did, when all His disciples fled at the time He was arrested. Especially Peter, who said He would go with him to the cross, now denied even knowing Him.

Jesus however, after He arose from the dead, sought out Peter, who along with the other disciples had gone back to their old trade, fishing, to express His unconditional love, John 21:15-17. I can imagine how ashamed and embarrassed Peter must have felt when he saw Jesus again. Take note here that love goes out of its way to restore the offender. It was Jesus who went to find Peter! He did not wait for Peter to come to Him.

Jesus prepared fish and bread for them to dine together. I can imagine how petrified they were as He broke bread and gave them fish to eat to refresh them from the long toil they had on the ocean that night.

After they had eaten, Jesus spoke directly to Peter, who was still smarting from his own failure, just days before. Jesus asked Peter a very important question. "Peter do you love me?" Peter's responded, "Yes Lord, I love you" again Jesus asked the very same question and again Peter responded as before, "Yes, Lord I love you." Peter was sad that Jesus was asking him the same question another time and by this, he was sure Jesus knew the answer. Jesus was asking, "Do you Agape me?" Peter was responding, "Yes, I Phileo you."

Peter was distressed because He realized that mere flesh couldn't do Agape love. He tried it before and failed miserably in his denial of His Lord at the time He needed him most. He remembered how he swore that he would fight for the Lord prior to Jesus' arrest, but at the time when he should show up, he failed. Now Jesus is asking him if he Peter Agape Him. "He knows that I cannot Agape him, what is He asking of me?"

Jesus, in realizing that Peter could not at that time come up to His standard of Agape love, responded to what Peter had to offer instead. He asked him the question the third time, but this time he did not used 'Agape,' He asked, "Do you 'Phileo' me?"

Peter saw Agape love in action, demonstrated by the Master Teacher Himself. Not only by His unselfish act of love on Calvary, but that He went to find a broken disciple who could not find himself. Peter was humbled that Jesus, the Rabbi, would come to where he was. How could he have said, "I Agape you," when he could not stand, even before a slave girl, to acknowledge his Lord? He thought he understood that love, but he fell short. Philo is all he could offer for now: a deep, instinctive, personal affection as for a close friend. He would no longer make rash statements he could not back up.

Many of us have failed miserably at some point in our lives, and because of those past experiences have not allowed ourselves to receive the unconditional love of Christ in our life. It is therefore quite hard to give love to others if first we have not received it to ourselves. Just as Peter received God's love, I implore you to receive the love of Christ. His all-amazing love! When you have received God's divine love then you can go one in forgiving others.

Forgiveness must come through the womb of unconditional love; a love that will sacrifice all that others would go free. This love is only found in Christ as was confirmed by His death for us. Peter in the latter years of his life lived close in his love relationship with his Lord, that at the time of his death he chose to die on an upside down cross. He felt so unworthy of the One who taught him the greatest lessons in love. He grew in boldness and love towards others and towards God. Love is the evidence of our faith.

The Products of Love

The book of Galatians 5:22, speaks of love as a fruit of the Spirit. Love is the first spiritual virtue of the Spirit, thus a good fruit. A good fruit cannot come from a bad or corrupt tree according to Matthew 7:17, which states, "Likewise, every good tree bears good fruit, but a bad tree bears bad fruit." To bear good fruit we must constantly guard our hearts against evil thoughts that sometimes come through offense. We should seek constantly to grow in love towards others. The more love grows, the more mature we become in the Spirit. When we are matured in love it will not be as hard to love our enemies, because we are no longer living from the carnal nature and what its dictates.

What is the carnal nature? The life we live in the flesh. The flesh is carnal, it has no good deed generating from it. Its produce is nothing but undesirable deeds. It stores offence and keeps it ablaze through strife. It does not encourage peace or demonstrates love. Instead the carnal nature leads to spiritual death and a life away from God.

Paul sums it up like this in Galatians 5:16, "But I say, walk by the Spirit, and you will not carry out the desire of the flesh." The flesh is an enemy to the Spirit and likewise the Spirit to the flesh. They are constantly at war. The Spirit can only win the battle when we walk steadfast in Him, by adhering to His principles. The more we allow Him to govern our lives, the more the fruit of love is becoming evident. We cannot react to certain situations anymore as we once did, because the flesh is being put under subjection to the Spirit within us.

We will never be without the enemy's advances. The enemy will always be around. When the love of Christ is flowing from us though, we can love those whom the enemy uses against us. Jesus' admonished the disciples in Matthew 5:44, 45a, "But I say unto you, love your enemies and pray for those who persecute you that you may be son of your father who is in heaven." Love should be the core of our daily living. As you will notice, in Galatians 5:22, love is the first of the fruit. It is the wellspring from which the rest of the virtues overflow our lives: joy, peace, patience, kindness, goodness, faithfulness, gentleness and self-control. All these are the by-products of love. As we mature more in love these fruit become evident in our lives.

If we are to live in the Kingdom of Heaven, then we should endeavor to measure our lives according to the teaching of the word. Let us love in deed and not only in the time of need. If truly we love God then we must love our fellow man. John spoke of this in, 1 John 4:20, by saying, "If someone says, "I love God," and hates his brother, he is a liar; for the one who does not love his brother whom he has seen, cannot love God whom he has not seen." I concur that life does throw us a curve ball, hitting us so hard we sometimes stumble. Nevertheless, we must endeavor to get back up quickly, and endeavor not to allow bitterness to overpower or cripple the Spirit within. Forgive those whom you must through the power of love.

We have a rich heritage in Christ to follow. As we endeavor to walk like Him, then it demands that we must stay close to Him, following in His footsteps. Peter did not evolve overnight. He accepted his failures as such; he realized that he could not change what was done. He, however, did not allow his past failures and regrets to overpower the purpose God preordained for him. Instead he accepted the unconditional love of Christ and lived out the Kingdom life, from the perspective of unconditional love, thus securing a place in the annals of history as a martyr for Christ.

How about you? Peter's failure did not hinder his final outcome. Should you allow things from the past to cloudy your future? Are you living from the flesh or of the Spirit? The Spirit produces life, while the flesh produces spiritual death. Love is the fruit you just got to have! Be encouraged! Know that you too can be changed into becoming a proactive, productive citizen in the Kingdom of God. His grace will keep you even in the time when you feel you have messed up. Since this Kingdom foundation is erected on love, practice love on a daily basis. Give up the unnecessary, to gain that which is necessary...LOVE!

Chapter 6

*"As I walked out the door toward the gate that would lead to my
freedom, I knew if I didn't leave my bitterness and hatred behind, I'd
still be in prison."*
Nelson Mandela*

Door to Freedom!

Stephen Owens in his book, *Set Free*, told the story of how
he finds forgiveness for his mother, many years after finding his
father brutally murdered in their home in Memphis, Tennessee,
1986. [4] Several days later, his mother was arrested for the
murder and was later sentenced to death for hiring a hit man to
kill his father whom he adored. He, being only 12 years old at the
time, packed bitterness, resentment and unforgiveness in his
heart against her for the greater part of his life. He shared the
journey of how he walked through unforgiveness and the events
that led up to him finally making the decision to visit her on death
row. He shared what transpired from that point, to where he was
instrumental in her being removed from death row and later
released from prison.

Stephen wrote in detail about the manner of time it took
him to go visit his mother. Once that became a reality he heard
what he never thought he would hear, her asking his forgiveness.
He reciprocated by receiving the forgiveness she offered. Stephen
described what took place after, the freedom he felt on the inside.
He needed that release of forgiveness for him to "live" a life of
freedom. For him, his mother was still alive and he was able to
get that forgiveness issue settled. For many it is not so. The
offender has either died or has moved away. The forgiveness

issue still needs to be settled in your heart once and for all, whether the words or spoke or not.

I am quite aware that there are those who have gone through traumatic experiences such as incest, spousal abuse: physical, emotional and mental, many have lost loved ones by homicide. Back in history of slavery, in America, many black men were hanged, their women raped and their children taken. Families were left to deal with this insidious crimes and no one has apologized for what was done. Likewise, the Holocaust was an unimaginable atrocity to humankind, as thousands of Jews were either killed or died from diseases or starvation in concentration camps in Germany. Those who survived and their families were left with the pain and memory, scared forever.

These are indeed potent issues that have been strewn by the wayside of life which have caused deep wounds. Many are still "bent over" from carrying that burden for so long. Yet, although these crimes are quite horrible, painful and unimaginable by those of us, who have not walked in the moccasins of those who were hurt by it, the truth remains that forgiveness must be released in order for true freedom to take place. Forgiveness is the grace that must be released in order for the sweet fragrance of freedom to spring forth in our lives, giving one the will to live again.

June Hunt, in her book, *How to Forgive When You Don't Feel Like It*, talked about the cumbersome bag of "rocks" we carry, filled with "boulders of bitterness," and "heavy rocks of resentment" that have being weighing us down. [5] Many have been carrying these stones since childhood unto their adult years. We somehow manage to function in a fast paced world carrying these offences but far from living in true freedom.

Too many are living meaningless fearful lives enslaved by the past. Dark shadows seem to loom everywhere blocking the sunlight from their lives. Emptiness seems to prevail causing some to indulge in immorality or to wallow in self-pity, self-hatred and even depression. The reality though is that none of those behaviors have elevated you to a place of true permanent freedom. Therefore, it's time to recognize what rocks of offence you have been carrying, and do whatever possible to remove those offences from your life.

Steven Owen wrote about this in his book; how daily he had to walk out forgiveness for his mother. The choice she made impacted his life as well as that of his brother, for a lifetime. Nevertheless, in order for him to be free he made the choice to forgive her, and in doing so released himself from his own 'prison' of anger, rage, bitterness and resentment. Agreeable, the act of injustice that was done will never be forgotten but to be locked in the prison of the past is just as deadly as the act itself.

I have spoken to several who have asked, "Why do I have to be the one to forgive, when I did not do anything wrong?" or "If I forgive the person then I would appear weak or vulnerable?" The truth is you cannot be responsible for the behaviors of others, but you are choosing to forgive to set yourself free; to take back your life and to be released from your 'prison,' and thus optimum health. The person who had caused the offence is indeed responsible for his or her own behavior, but their lack of concern to ask forgiveness should not hinder you from being set free.

The question that should help you to move forward is, "How long will I remain dormant in this position?" or "Do I want to remain a victim forever?" This is your choice. Look at who you are, what you have endured. The fact that you are still here could only mean that you are already a winner! You are stronger than you can ever imagine. You might not feel as if you are, but after all that you have been through, you have guided the ship of your life through many deep waters, with the help of the Master of the ocean, and has survived. Refuse to be a victim any longer and become the victor, the person who has overcome. The prison door is now open...

The Grace to Forgive:

Years ago, I remember reading the story of Corrie Ten Boom, a survivor of the Holocaust whose father and sister both died in one of the concentration camps in Ravensbruck, Germany. Corrie miraculously was released from concentration camp because of a clerical error. She had the privilege to share her story and that of the countless others who suffered the greatest atrocity against mankind. June Hunt in her book, "*How To Forgive When You Don't Feel Like It*," recapped the story of Corrie Ten Boom and how she forgave those who had perpetrated such terrible crimes against the Jewish people.

In one of her meetings in Munich, after speaking about forgiveness Corrie related the story of how her forgiveness was tested. This is Corrie's story: "That's when I saw him, working his way forward against the others. One moment I saw the overcoat and the brown hat; the next, a blue uniform and a visored cap with its skull and crossbones.

It came back with a rush: the huge room with its harsh overhead lights; the pathetic pile of dresses and shoes in the center of the floor; the shame of walking naked past this man. I could see my sister's frail form ahead of me, ribs sharp beneath the parchment skin. Betsie, how thin you were! The place was Ravensbruck, and the man who was making his way forward had been a guard—one of the most cruel guards.

Now he was in front of me, hand thrust out. "A fine message, Fraulein! How good it is to know that, as you say, all our sins are at the bottom of the sea!" And I, who had spoken so glibly of forgiveness, fumbled in my pocketbook rather than take that hand.

He would not remember me, of course—how could he remember one prisoner among those thousands of women? But I remembered him and the leather crop swinging from his belt. I was face-to-face with one of my captors and my blood seemed to freeze

"You mentioned Ravensbruck in your talk…. I was a guard there…. But since that time, I have become a Christian. I know that God has forgiven me for the cruel things I did there, but I would like to hear it from your lips as well. Fraulein,"—again, the hand came out—"will you forgive me?" Corrie described her frenzy of thoughts and emotions: I stood there—I whose sins had again and again had been forgiven—and could not forgive.

Betsie had died in that place—could he erase her slow terrible death simply for the asking? It could not have been many seconds that he stood there—hand held out—but to me it seemed hours as I wrestled with the most difficult thing I ever had to do. For I had to do it—I knew that.

The message that God forgives has a prior condition: that we forgive those who have injured us. "If you do not forgive men their trespasses," Jesus says, "neither will your Father in heaven forgive your trespasses."…And still I stood there with the coldness clutching my heart. But forgiveness is not an emotion—I knew that too. Forgiveness is an act of the will, and the will can function regardless of the temperature of the heart. "Jesus, help me!" I prayed silently. "I can lift my hand. I can do that much. You supply the feeling." And so woodenly, mechanically, I thrust my hand into the one stretched out to me. And as I did, an incredible thing took place.

The current started in my shoulder, raced down my arm, sprang into our joined hands. And then the healing warmth seemed to flood my whole being, bringing tears to my eyes. "I forgive you, brother!" I cried. "With all my heart!" For a long moment, we grasped each other's hands, the former guard and the former prisoner. Corrie later wrote, "I had never known God's love so intensely, as I did then. But even so, I realized it was not my love. I had tried, and did not have the power. It was the power of the Holy Spirit."

Corrie, although lecturing about forgiveness, on seeing the man who was actually responsible for the death of thousands, including her sister and her father, had to make the choice of a lifetime to forgive him fully from the heart. Oh, what blessed freedom when true forgiveness is assured. The prison door is open and the prisoner is set free. Like Corrie, God will show you another hurdle that you must thrust through and another. Each time it gets better until your life becomes one of walking in forgiveness. As we expect to receive forgiveness, so we too must demonstrate true forgiveness to others.

Chapter 7

If you don't like something, change it. If you can't change it, change
your attitude.
Maya Angelou

The Toxic Effect of Unforgiveness

In the last several chapters, we have been looking at unforgiveness from a spiritual perspective, seeing how it can damage our spirit, our relationships with each other as well as with the Creator. In this chapter we will look at unforgiveness from the medical point-of-view and the short and long-term effect it has on the physical body, and what we can do to bring our body back in proper alignment with healthier living.

More and more doctors are linking the effect of unforgiveness with chronic health issues. In one article written by Dr. Sheryl Luskin she said this: "Lack of forgiveness, which often occurs as a result of having been hurt, humiliated, angered, or having suffered fear or loss, feelings of guilt, or envy, can have profound effects on the way your body functions. [6]

Physically the body is in a state of stress. Muscles tighten, causing imbalances or pain in the neck, back and limbs. Blood flow to the joints is restricted, making it more difficult for the blood to remove wastes from the tissues and reducing the supply of oxygen and nutrients to the cells. Normal processes of repair and recovery from injury or arthritis are impaired. Clenching of the jaws contributes to problems with teeth and jaw joints. Headaches can become a problem. Chronic pain may get worse.

Blood flow to the heart is constricted. Digestion is impaired. Breathing may become more difficult. Anger can seriously impair the immune system, increasing the risk of infections and illness.

Luskin cites several studies that show how anger can affect the cardiovascular system by adding to a person's general level of stress. Other studies have indicated that patients who have had heart attacks have been able to improve their physical health by practicing forgiveness and working to feel more tolerant and less angry.

Additionally, Dr. Luskin says, "When the body releases certain enzymes during anger and stress, cholesterol and blood pressure levels go up, not a good long-term position to put the body in. Forgiveness has been shown to lower blood pressure naturally. The bottom line, we can eat healthy and take care of ourselves on a physical level, but if our hearts are filled with anger, our bodies are not in optimum health." [5]

Stress and the Body

Dr. Luskin, in her article, refers to "anger and stress." In almost every article I have reviewed, the word stress looms from the pages. Stress plays a major part in all illnesses. So the question would be what is stress? Stress is physiological, meaning a specific response by the body to a stimulus, as fear or pain that disturbs or interferes with the normal physiological equilibrium of an organism. It is also physical, mental or emotional strain or tension; worry, anxiety, burden, pressure, oppression, exertion or struggle, etc. In looking at the definition and synonyms of stress, we definitely can conclude that unforgiveness is a stressor.

According to a study done by Brock University, Mental Health division, Stress can be described in two categories: Eustress, which is positive stress, and one which motivates us to get something done. Most people work well with this stress. It's this same type of stress that we might experience on a regular basis when something good is accomplished such as saving to buy a new car. Distress, on the other hand, is the negative stress and the ones that we refer to the most. "It is when this stress is no longer tolerable and/or manageable that distress comes in.

Bad stress, or distress, is when the good stress becomes too much to bear or cope with. Tension builds, there is no longer any fun in the challenge, there seems to be no relief, no end in sight. This is the kind of stress most of us are familiar with and this is the kind of stress that leads to poor decision making." [7]

We can view eustress and distress in relation to a woman who is expecting her first child. She is ecstatic with joy; she walks around in a state of euphoria, awaiting the arrival of the child, positive stress. After the child was born however, she found that her baby was born with an unexpected illness. Soon euphoria turns into distress as she becomes overwhelmed and tired. The positive stress now has become negative stress. If she stays in this distress for a very long period of time her entire being will begin to feel the impact. Similarly, when we stay in unforgiveness for long length of time it will definitely affect, not only our body but even our thinking becomes vague and uncertain.

Stress and the Mind

It is essential that every individual understand the responsibility he or she has to his or her body. An unhealthy, mind, spirit or body cannot function to the maximum capacity. Years ago there was a commercial, which said, "The mind is a terrible thing to waste." This is quite true. We need a healthy mind to function. Stress affects the mind as much as it does the physical body. Putting too many unhealthy and negative thoughts in the mind on a daily basis is just as deadly. Often times we cannot understand why we are sad, anxious or irritated in our minds; we cannot identify any conscious things that are producing such reaction. The reason could be some irksome, negative things that have been tucked away in the sub or unconscious mind that need to be identified and scrubbed clean.

I once heard the story of a young man who would not forgive anyone who had done him wrong. He chose not to accept the apology of any who might have offended him. He plainly refused to forgive whether family, friends or foe. He developed certain health issues and after several tests were done, he was diagnosed with cancer. Where he had the cancer was what was frightening. He died not much longer from cancer of the heart. How much easier it would have been to forgive and release that toxic poison of bitterness, resentment and unforgiveness from his heart? Isn't it ironic that the very place where the toxic poison of unforgiveness was stored became cancerous and led to his death?

Truly, I am aware that many reading this book have gone through severe challenges, testing and trials unimaginable. In no way am I suggesting that forgiveness is easy, a cut and dry process; to some the process takes a little longer than others. We see that with Stephen Owens, his forgiving is mother took some time; in the case of the Amish community however, it was immediate. What is suggested here is: in order for you to be liberated and to live a long healthy and productive life it is necessary to practice the art of forgiveness.

Since medical doctors are citing correlations between unforgiveness and health issues, it might be a good time to take a look at your life, your health, mental and spiritual, to be sure there are not open access to the enemy. It's time to rid unforgiveness from you. If holding on to it has not benefited you in any way, then, it is time to start a new. It is time to enter through the door that brings true peace. Yes, the incident did happen! The pain is real, but now it is time to be free from the prison you are in.

If you are reading this book and have never prayed and asked Jesus in your heart, now is as good a time as any to do so.

"Father I realize that I am a sinner and I recognize that you are the Savior of the world. Please forgive me of all my sins, wash and cleanse me of all unrighteousness. I repent from all the anger, resentment and unforgiveness that I have harbored in my heart against others. Please teach me how to be more like you everyday, in Jesus name amen!!!

My Declaration

I declare today, that I am free from every entanglement of unforgiveness that has plagued my life. I choose to forgive everyone who has ever hurt, used or abused me. I declare that no sickness shall come upon my body because I harbored unforgiveness in my heart towards others. I renounce every trace of bitterness, resentments, jealousy, malice, evil thoughts, or any other negative thing from my mind. I refuse, any longer, to give anyone control over my life. I take my life back!! I choose life over death, light over darkness and forgiveness over unforgiveness. I will be the master of what goes in and out of my heart. I will guard my heart from evil; I declare that my mind is free to think good positive thoughts, and my mouth will speak good things...This I declare!

Healing Scriptures

Here are some of the Scriptures that helped me in the process I went through that first night.

Isaiah 40:28-31

Have you not known? Have you not heard? The everlasting God, the LORD, the Creator of the ends of the earth, neither faints nor is weary. His understanding is unsearchable. He gives power to the weak, and to those who have no might He increases strength. Even the youths shall faint and be weary, and the young men shall utterly fall, but those who wait on the LORD shall renew their strength; They shall mount up with wings like eagles, they shall run and not be weary, they shall walk and not faint.

Isaiah 41:10-14

"Fear not, for I am with you; be not dismayed, for I am your God. I will strengthen you, Yes, I will help you, I will uphold you with My righteous right hand. Behold, all those who were incensed against you shall be ashamed and disgraced; they shall be as nothing, and those who strive with you shall perish. You shall seek them and not find them - those who contended with you. Those who war against you shall be as nothing, as a nonexistent thing. For I, the LORD your God, will hold your right hand, saying to you, 'Fear not, I will help you.' Fear not, you worm Jacob, You men of Israel! I will help you," says the LORD And your Redeemer, the Holy One of Israel.

Isaiah 43:1-5

But now, thus says the LORD, who created you, O Jacob, and He who formed you, O Israel: "Fear not, for I have redeemed you;

I have called you by your name; You are Mine. When you pass through the waters, I will be with you; And through the rivers, they shall not overflow you. When you walk through the fire, you shall not be burned, nor shall the flame scorch you. For I am the LORD your God, The Holy One of Israel, your Savior; I gave Egypt for your ransom, Ethiopia and Seba in your place. Since you were precious in My sight, You have been honored, and I have loved you; therefore I will give men for you, and people for your life. Fear not, for I am with you; I will bring your descendants from the east, And gather you from the west."

Isaiah 45:2-3

I will go before you and make the crooked places straight; I will break in pieces the gates of bronze and cut the bars of iron. I will give you the treasures of darkness and hidden riches of secret places, that you may know that I, the LORD, who call you by your name, Am the God of Israel.

Isaiah 46:4

Even to your old age, I am He, and even to gray hairs I will carry you! I have made, and I will bear; even I will carry, and will deliver you.

Isaiah 54:1-17

"Sing, O barren, you who have not borne! Break forth into singing, and cry aloud, you who have not labored with child! For more are the children of the desolate than the children of the married woman," says the LORD. "Enlarge the place of your tent, and let them stretch out the curtains of your dwellings; do not spare; lengthen your cords, and strengthen your stakes. For you shall expand to the right and to the left, and your descendants will inherit the nations, and make the desolate cities inhabited."

[4] "Do not fear, for you will not be ashamed; neither be disgraced, for you will not be put to shame; for you will forget the shame of your youth, and will not remember the reproach of your

widowhood anymore. For your Maker is your husband, The LORD of hosts is His name; and your Redeemer is the Holy One of Israel; he is called the God of the whole earth. For the LORD has called you like a woman forsaken and grieved in spirit, like a youthful wife when you were refused," says your God. "For a mere moment I have forsaken you, but with great mercies I will gather you. With a little wrath I hid My face from you for a moment; but with everlasting kindness I will have mercy on you," says the LORD, your Redeemer.

[9] "For this is like the waters of Noah to Me; for as I have sworn that the waters of Noah would no longer cover the earth, so have I sworn that I would not be angry with you, nor rebuke you. For the mountains shall depart and the hills be removed, but My kindness shall not depart from you, nor shall My covenant of peace be removed," says the LORD, who has mercy on you.

[11] "O you afflicted one, tossed with tempest, and not comforted, behold, I will lay your stones with colorful gems, and lay your foundations with sapphires. I will make your pinnacles of rubies, your gates of crystal, and all your walls of precious stones. All your children shall be taught by the LORD, and great shall be the peace of your children. In righteousness you shall be established; you shall be far from oppression, for you shall not fear; and from terror, for it shall not come near you. Indeed they shall surely assemble, but not because of Me. Whoever assembles against you shall fall for your sake.

[16] "Behold, I have created the blacksmith who blows the coals in the fire, who brings forth an instrument for his work; and I have created the spoiler to destroy. No weapon formed against you shall prosper, and every tongue which rises against you in judgment You shall condemn. This is the heritage of the servants of the LORD, And their righteousness is from Me," says the LORD.

Forgiveness Scriptures

Luke 17:3-4

Take heed to yourselves. If your brother sins against you, rebuke him; and if he repents, forgive him. And if he sins against you seven times in a day, and seven times in a day returns to you, saying, 'I repent,' you shall forgive him."

Matthew 18:15-20

"Moreover if your brother sins against you, go and tell him his fault between you and him alone. If he hears you, you have gained your brother. But if he will not hear, take with you one or two more, that 'by the mouth of two or three witnesses every word may be established.' And if he refuses to hear them, tell it to the church. But if he refuses even to hear the church, let him be to you like a heathen and a tax collector. "Assuredly, I say to you, whatever you bind on earth will be bound in heaven, and whatever you loose on earth will be loosed in heaven.

"Again I say to you that if two of you agree on earth concerning anything that they ask, it will be done for them by My Father in heaven. For where two or three are gathered together in My name, I am there in the midst of them."

Ephesians 4:32

Let all bitterness, wrath, anger, clamor, and evil speaking be put away from you, with all malice. And be kind to one another, tenderhearted, forgiving one another, even as God in Christ forgave you.

Colossians 2:13-14

And you, being dead in your trespasses and the uncircumcision of your flesh, He has made alive together with Him, having forgiven you all trespasses, having wiped out the handwriting of requirements that was against us, which was contrary to us. And He has taken it out of the way, having nailed it to the cross.

Colossians 3:15-16

Therefore, as the elect of God, holy and beloved, put on tender mercies, kindness, humility, meekness, longsuffering; bearing with one another, and forgiving one another, if anyone has a complaint against another; even as Christ forgave you, so you also must do. But above all these things put on love, which is the bond of perfection.

Daily Kingdom Check-Up

Here are five ways to determine whether you are holding unforgiveness in your heart.

    (1) Is there fever of anger?
    (2) Is there any chill of malice?
    (3) Is there any pain of unforgiveness?
    (4) Is there any aching from lovelessness?
    (5) Is there any apathy or lack of concern about sins in your life?

Indicators of Unforgiveness.

    (1) Inability to forgive yourself.
    (2) Crying in silence.
    (3) Constantly rehearsing and reviving the painful memories of the offense to other people.
    (4) Holding on to the Victim and Prey Mentality.
    (5) Seeking self-pity.
    (6) Having no peace in your life.
    (7) Some poor health conditions, including stress, illnesses as arthritis, certain cancers, joint pains or chronic pains, inflammations, migraines, stroke, and heart problems.

How to overcome unforgiveness.

(1) Forgiving yourself first.
(2) Forgive the person(s) who have offended or injured you.
(3) Identify any sin in your life and renounce it.
(4) Choose well the person you call your counselor or advisor; avoid negative people. Positive reinforcement is needed to help you gain back control over the problem.
(5) Put on the character of Christ, by growing in true and unconditional love and extending it to everyone.

Results of forgiving the offender.

(1) You will have a good relationship with God.
(2) You will have a good relationship with other people, including your spouse, children and parents.
(3) You will live life of true freedom; the enemy will not have control or power over your life.
(4) You will walk in divine health.
(5) You will become a proactive and productive citizen in the Kingdom of God.

"When you hold resentment toward another, you are bound to that person or condition by an emotional link that is stronger than steel. Forgiveness is the only way to dissolve that link and get free." – Catherine Ponder.

Bibliography

(1) Collins Gem Dictionary

(2) *Amish Grace*, Lifetime Movie presentation, March 28, 2010

(3) Wikipedia

(4) Owens, Stephen; Abraham, Ken (2013-09-05). Set Free: Discover Forgiveness Amidst Murder and Betrayal. B&H Publishing Group. Kindle Edition.

(5) Hunt, June (2007-09-01). How to Forgive...When You Don't Feel Like It (p. 57-60). Harvest House Publishers. Kindle Edition.

(6) Linskin, Sheryl; Natural News Health News and Science Discovery.

(7) Stress; Brock University 50; (1964-2014) Mental Health

30995024R00044

Made in the USA
Charleston, SC
03 July 2014